G000293548

20 CLASSICAL THEMES

- Air on the G String
- Ave Maria
- Brahm's Lullaby
- Canon in D
- Dido's Lament
- Eine Kleine Nachtmusik
- Funeral March
- Fur Elise
- Hallelujah from Messiah
- In the Hall of the Mountain King
- Jupiter from the Planets
- Largo
- Ode to Joy
- Pavane
- Pomp and Circumstance
- Sleeping Beauty Waltz
- Spring from the Four Seasons
- The Blue Danube
- The Sorcerer's Apprentice
- Trumpet Voluntary

ARRANGED BY B. C. DOCKERY

WWW.BENDOCKERY.COM

Copyright © 2023 B. C. Dockery

All rights reserved.

Because this is a single bound book, photocopies are permitted for performance purposes only.

Air on the G String

J. S. Bach
arr. B. C. Dockery

©2021

Air on the G String

Cello I

J. S. Bach
arr. B. C. Dockery

©2021

Air on the G String

J. S. Bach
arr. B. C. Dockery

Piano

©2021

Air on the G String

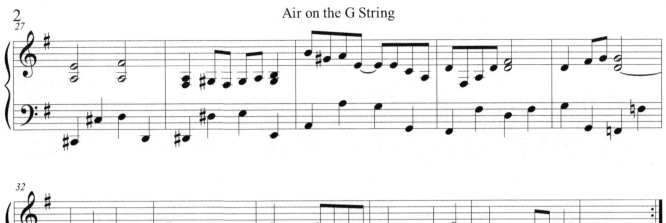

Ave Maria

Score

Franz Schubert

B. C. Dockery

©2023

poco rit.

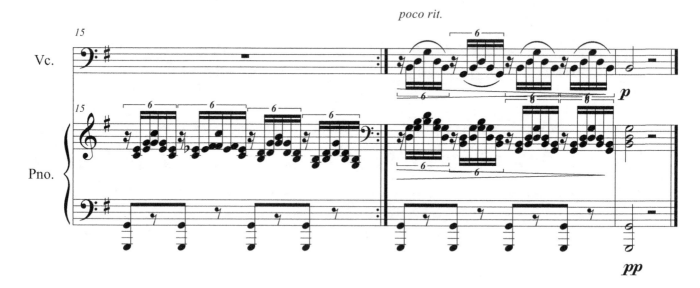

Ave Maria

Cello 1

Franz Schubert
B. C. Dockery

poco rit.

©2023

Ave Maria

Piano

Franz Schubert
B. C. Dockery

©2023

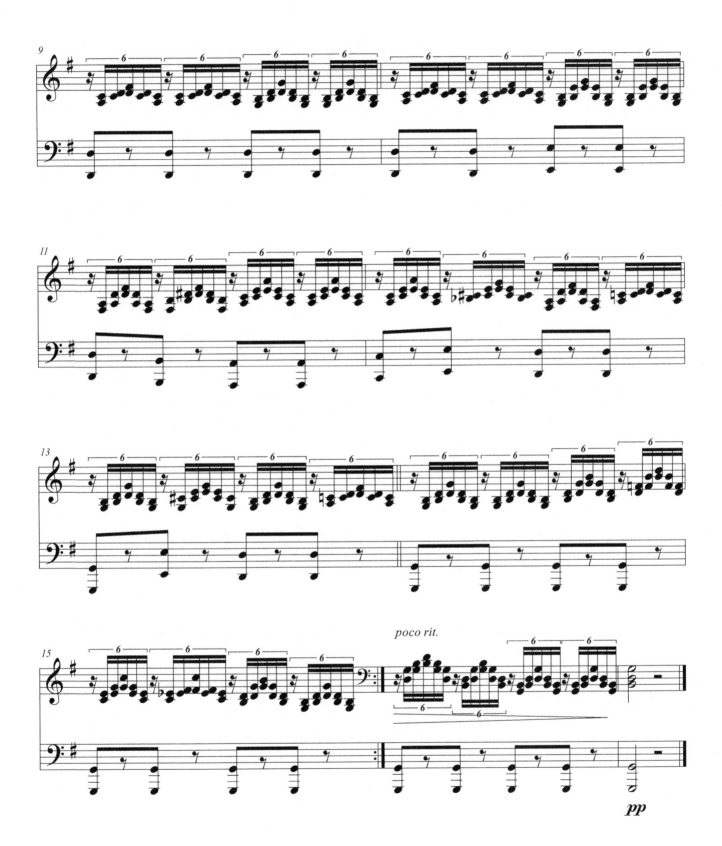

Lullaby

Wiegenlied

Johannes Brahms
B. C. Dockery

©2023

Lullaby

Lullaby
Wiegenlied

Cello 1

Johannes Brahms
B. C. Dockery

©2023

Lullaby
Wiegenlied

Piano

Johannes Brahms
B. C. Dockery

©2023

Canon in D

Johann Pachelbel
arr. B. C. Dockery

©2021

Canon in D

Canon in D

Canon in D

Canon in D

Cello I

Johann Pachelbel
arr. B. C. Dockery

©2021

Canon in D

Canon in D

Piano

Johann Pachelbel
arr. B. C. Dockery

©2021

Canon in D

Canon in D

Dido's Lament

from Dido and Aeneas

Henry Purcell
B. C. Dockery

Larghetto ♩ = 56

©2023

Cello 1

Dido's Lament
from Dido and Aeneas

Henry Purcell
B. C. Dockery

Larghetto ♩ = 56

©2023

Piano

Dido's Lament
from Dido and Aeneas

Henry Purcell
B. C. Dockery

Larghetto ♩ = 56

©2023

Score

Eine Kleine Nachtmusik

K. 525 First Movement
First Theme

Wolfgang Amadeus Mozart

B. C. Dockery

©2023

Eine Kleine Nachtmusik

K. 525 First Movement
First Theme

Cello

Wolfgang Amadeus Mozart
B. C. Dockery

©2023

Eine Kleine Nachtmusik

K. 525 First Movement
First Theme

Piano

Wolfgang Amadeus Mozart

B. C. Dockery

©2023

Funeral March

Score

Frederic Chopin
B. C. Dockery

©2023

Funeral March

Cello 1

Frederic Chopin
B. C. Dockery

©2023

Funeral March

Piano

Frederic Chopin
B. C. Dockery

©2023

Fur Elise

Score

Beethoven
B. C. Dockery

©2023

Fur Elise

Vc.

Vc.

Fur Elise

Cello 1

Beethoven
B. C. Dockery

©2023

Fur Elise

Piano

Beethoven
B. C. Dockery

©2023

Hallelujah Chorus

From Messiah

Score

George Frederick Handel

B. C. Dockery

©2023

Hallelujah Chorus

From Messiah

Cello 1

George Frederick Handel
B. C. Dockery

©2023

Hallelujah Chorus
From Messiah

Piano

George Frederick Handel
B. C. Dockery

©2023

In the Hall of the Mountain King

Score

From Peer Gynt

Edvard Grieg
B. C. Dockery

©2023

In the Hall of the Mountain King

In the Hall of the Mountain King

Cello 1

From Peer Gynt

Edvard Grieg

B. C. Dockery

©2023

In the Hall of the Mountain King

Piano

From Peer Gynt

Edvard Grieg

B. C. Dockery

accelerando

©2023

Jupiter

from The Planets

Gustav Holst

B. C. Dockery

©2023

Jupiter

Jupiter
from The Planets

Cello 1

Gustav Holst
B. C. Dockery

©2023

Jupiter
from The Planets

Piano

Gustav Holst

B. C. Dockery

©2023

Goin' Home
Largo from New World Symphony

Score

Traditional
Antonin Dvorak
B. C. Dockery

©2023

Goin' Home

Goin' Home
Largo from New World Symphony

Cello 1

Traditional
Antonin Dvorak
B. C. Dockery

©2023

Goin' Home
Largo from New World Symphony

Piano

Traditional
Antonin Dvorak
B. C. Dockery

©2023

Goin' Home

Ode to Joy
(Joyful, Joyful, We Adore Thee)

Beethoven
arr. B. C. Dockery

©2021

Ode to Joy
(Joyful, Joyful, We Adore Thee)

Ode to Joy
(Joyful, Joyful, We Adore Thee)

Cello

Beethoven
arr. B. C. Dockery

Moderately

©2021

Ode to Joy
(Joyful, Joyful, We Adore Thee)

Piano

Beethoven
arr. B. C. Dockery

Moderately

©2021

Pavane

Score

Gabriel Faure

B. C. Dockery

©2023

Pavane

Cello 1

Gabriel Faure
B. C. Dockery

©2023

Pavane

Piano

Gabriel Faure
B. C. Dockery

©2023

Pomp and Circumstance
March No. 1

Edward Elgar
B. C. Dockery

Score

©2023

Pomp and Circumstance
March No. 1

Pomp and Circumstance
March No. 1

Edward Elgar
B. C. Dockery

Cello 1

©2023

Pomp and Circumstance
March No. 1

Edward Elgar
B. C. Dockery

Piano

©2023

Sleeping Beauty Waltz

Score

Tchaikovsky
B. C. Dockery

©2023

Sleeping Beauty Waltz

Cello 1

Tchaikovsky
B. C. Dockery

©2023

Sleeping Beauty Waltz

Piano

Tchaikovsky
B. C. Dockery

©2023

Spring from the Four Seasons

Antonio Vivaldi
arr. B. C. Dockery

©2021

Spring from the Four Seasons

Spring from the Four Seasons

Cello 1

Antonio Vivaldi
arr. B. C. Dockery

©2021

Spring from the Four Seasons

Piano

Antonio Vivaldi
arr. B. C. Dockery

©2021

Spring from the Four Seasons

Score

On the Beautiful Blue Danube

Johann Strauss, Jr.
B. C. Dockery

©2023

D.C. al Fine

Cello 1

On the Beautiful Blue Danube

Johann Strauss, Jr.

B. C. Dockery

©2023

Piano

On the Beautiful Blue Danube

Johann Strauss, Jr.
B. C. Dockery

©2023

The Sorcerer's Apprentice

Score

Paul Dukas

B. C. Dockery

©2023

The Sorcerer's Apprentice

Cello 1

Paul Dukas

B. C. Dockery

©2023

The Sorcerer's Apprentice

Piano

Paul Dukas

B. C. Dockery

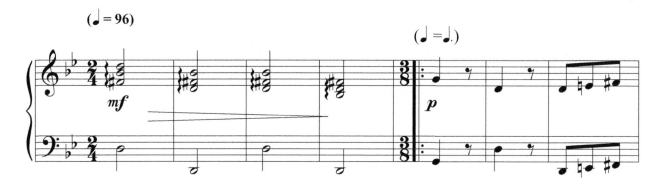

©2023

Trumpet Voluntary

Jeremy Clark
arr. B. C. Dockery

©2021

Trumpet Voluntary

Cello 1

Jeremy Clark
arr. B. C. Dockery

©2021

Trumpet Voluntary

Piano

Jeremy Clark
arr. B. C. Dockery

©2021

Trumpet Voluntary

Printed in Great Britain
by Amazon

42267016R00071